STAGE
3
BOOK 4

COOK OF THE YEAR

John Townsend

Riverside Primary School

Janeway Street
SE16 4PS
Telephone 020 7237 3227 • Facsimile 020 7237 0047

RISING STARS

It was Cook of the Year night in Dockside. It was like a show on TV. JJ and Maya had to cook the meals.

"Our cooking is fit for a king," joked JJ.
"But no royal oysters today," Maya said with a grin.

JJ fried fish in oil. Maya boiled beef in beer. The room was filling with steam.

Can you put tin foil over the dish of peas, Miss Evans?

We're nearly set to go.

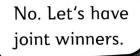

CHECK

1. Who were the cooks in 'Cook of the Year'?

2. What food did they cook?

3. Who ate the food?

4. How many marks did each of the cooks get?

5. Who was the winner?

FIND

Find the words to fill the gaps.

1. JJ and Maya had to _____ the meals. (page 2)

2. JJ _____ fish in oil.   (page 7)

3. Maya _____ beef in beer.   (page 7)

What's missing?

1. it was like a show on tv   (page 2)

2. our cooking is fit for a king joked jj   (page 3)

3. but no royal oysters today maya said with a grin
(page 3)

*Put the **nouns** (cooks, meals, food) in the right gaps.*

1. JJ and Maya had to cook the _____.   (page 2)

2. We'll enjoy your _____.   (page 5)

3. Miss Evans peered at the _____.   (page 6)